SAFARI READERS

BOOK STAGE 1

WolveS

SAFARI
READERS

Tristan WalterS

For Billy & Phoebe

- the original Safari Readers!

Copyright © 2019 Safari Readers

www.safarireaders.com

Written & Designed by Tristan Walters

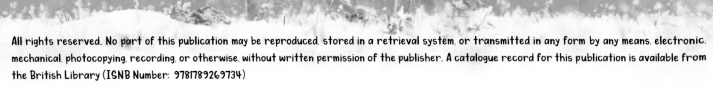

Acknowledgements [Key: DT - Dreamstime; FVM - FreeVectorMaps.com; SS - Shutterstock.com] Cover (background), Nattle/SS; Cover (middle), Szczepan Klejbuk/SS; 1, Michal Ninger/SS; 2-3, 26, Vlada Cech/SS; 4, Volodymyr Burdiak/SS; 6-7 (background), hslergrl/PX; 6-7 (middle), Mariait/SS; 8, Frenchwildlifephotographer/SS; 9 (top), carlosobriganti/SS; 9 (middle), Facanv/SS; 9 (bottom), Anya Newrcha/SS; 10-11 (background), Chiara Salvadori/SS; 12, Jan Havlicek/DT; 13, 23, FreeVectorMaps/FVM; 14, mlorenz/SS; 16-17, Frenchwildlifephotographer/SS; 18, Geoffrey Kuchera/SS; 20, Bildagentaur Zoonar GmbH/SS; 21 (top right), Alexey Sanchuk/SS; 21 (middle), Bildagentaur Zoonar GmbH/SS; 21 (bottom) Critterbiz/SS; 26, arbit/SS; Back (bottom left), Cyo Bo/SS. Animation Images (Back, 5, 7, 9-10, 15, 19, 23-28), Memo Angeles/SS.

Contents

What is a wolf? 4

What does a wolf look like? 6

Where do wolves live? 8

Why do wolves howl? 14

How many wolves live in a pack? 16

What do wolves eat? 18

What does a wolf pup look like? 20

Why are wolves in trouble? 22

Wolf puzzle 24

Glossary 28

What is a wolf?

A wolf is a big dog.

red fox

jackal

dingo

hunting dog

What other dogs can you see?

What does a wolf look like?

WOLF

 SCIENTIFIC NAME
Canis lupus

 SIZE
Up to 1.6m long

 WEIGHT
Up to 80 kg

 SPEED
60 km per hour

 AGE
Up to 15 years

fur

tail

paws

6

Where do wolves live?

forest

mountains

Arctic

desert

Did you know? Wolves have different fur to match their habitat.

Can you name each of the wolf **habitats**?

Wolves live in lots of places.

Where do wolves live?

eagle

YELLOWSTONE
NATIONAL PARK

 LOCATION
USA, North America

 HABITAT
Pine forests and grasslands

 SIZE
9,000 km²

bison

sheep

otter

Where do wolves live?

North America

Europe

Asia

Africa

South America

Oceania

N

= wolf habitat

What keeps you warm in the cold?

Wolves have thick fur to live in the cold.

Why do wolves howl?

Did you know?
Wolves howl to each other to send messages across their **territory**.

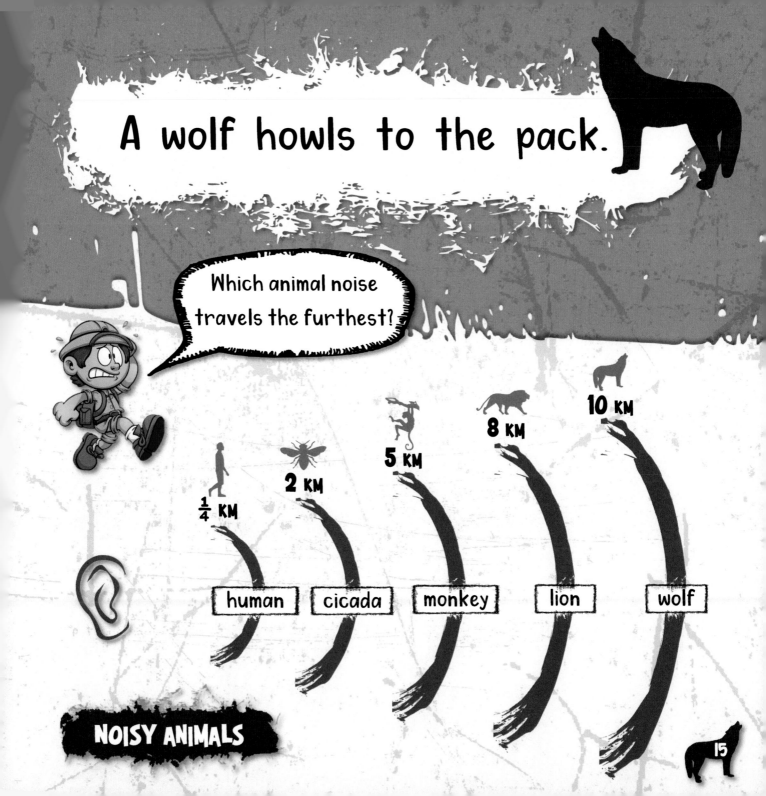

How many wolves
live in a pack?

A pack can have up to ten wolves.

What do wolves eat?

Did you know?
Wolves are **carnivores** and only eat meat from animals.

What does a wolf pup look like?

Wolf pups live in a den.

listening

watching

cuddling

Did you know?
Only the top or **alpha** wolves in a pack have pups.

hiding

Why are wolves in trouble?

Extinct	Extinct in the Wild	Critically Endangered	Endangered	Vulnerable	Near Threatened	Least Concern

CONSERVATION STATUS

Where wolves live

Where wolves used to live

What has happened to the wolf's range?

Wolves have been hunted lots in the past.

23

Wolf Puzzle

PUZZLE 1

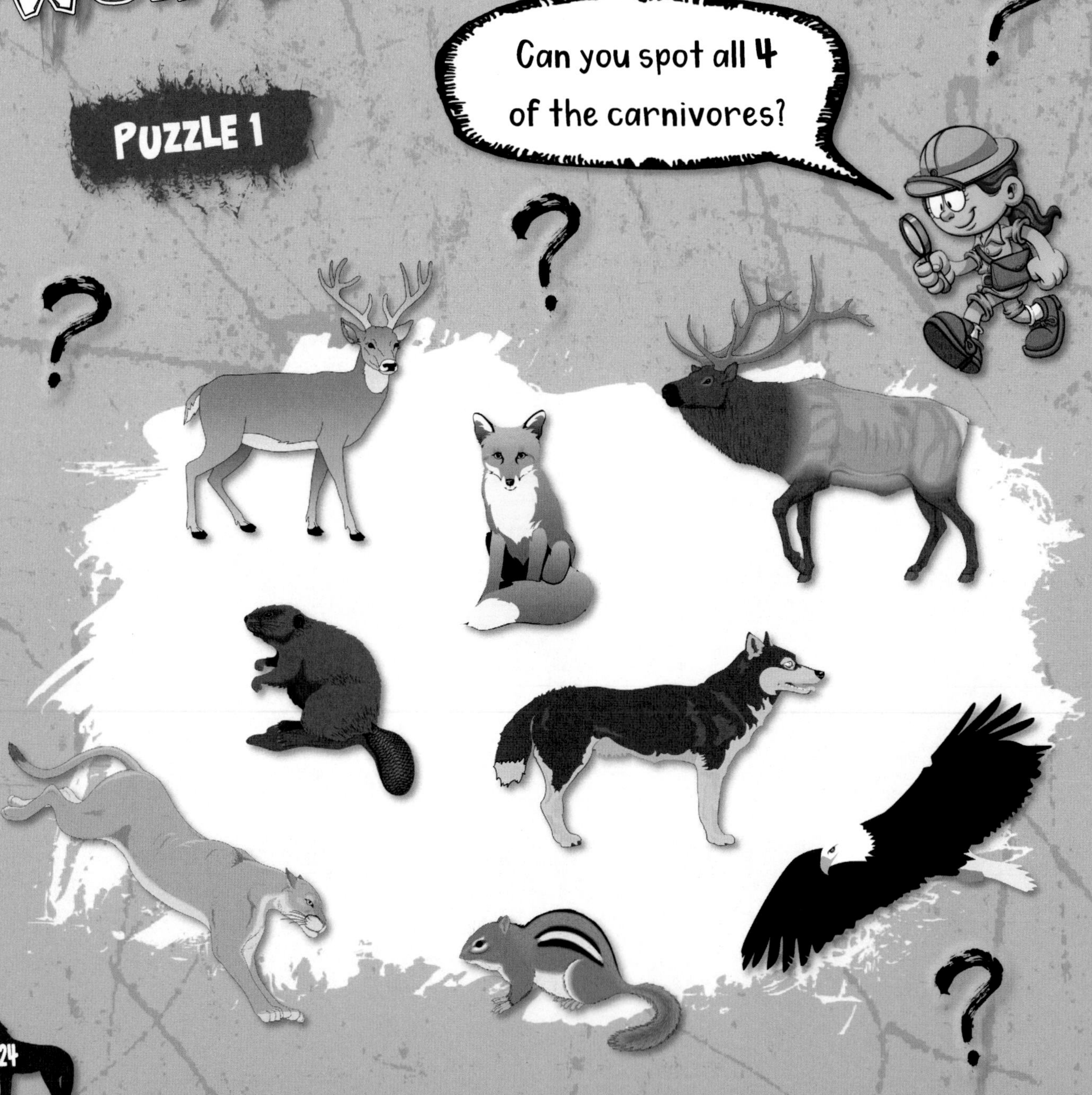

PUZZLE 2

Can you spot all **5** of the differences?

25

Safari Readers

The 'Safari Readers' books are specially designed to help children learn to read. Based on leading teaching practice, this series enables children to develop a range of reading skills and create a love of reading and language through wild and exciting topics.

Enjoy the ride!

Reading is fun! These books are best enjoyed when reading together.

The smaller text can be read by whoever is supporting the child.

The larger text is for the child to read.

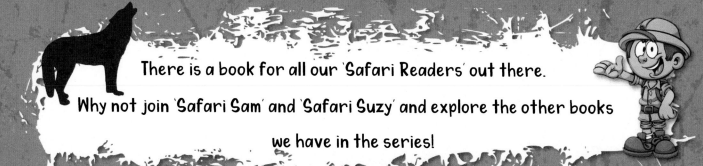

There is a book for all our 'Safari Readers' out there.

Why not join 'Safari Sam' and 'Safari Suzy' and explore the other books we have in the series!

STAGE 1

Cheetahs ☐
Flamingos ☐
Wolves ☑
Giraffes ☐
Dolphins ☐

STAGE 2

Sea Turtles ☐
Tigers ☐
Elephants ☐
Polar Bears ☐
Gorillas ☐

STAGE 3

Sharks ☐
Lions ☐
Penguins ☐
Snakes ☐
Monkeys ☐

For more information check out our website:

WWW.SAFARIREADERS.COM

Glossary

Can you remember all of the new words we have learnt?

Webbed when an animal has a layer of skin between its fingers or toes.

Habitat the area or place where an animal lives.

Territory an area of land that an animal or group lives in that is protected from others.

Carnivore an animal that eats only meat.

Alpha an animal that is in charge of a group.

Made in the USA
Middletown, DE
26 March 2020